Communication Skills for Leaders

Delivering a Clear and Consistent Message

Third Edition

Bert Decker

A Crisp Fifty-Minute™ Series Book

This Fifty-Minute™ Book is designed to be "read with a pencil." It is an excellent workbook for self-study as well as classroom learning. All material is copyright-protected and cannot be duplicated without permission from the publisher. *Therefore, be sure to order a copy for every training participant through our Web site, www.courseilt.com.*

Communication Skills for Leaders

Delivering a Clear and Consistent Message

Third Edition

Bert Decker

CREDITS:

Product Manager:	**Debbie Woodbury**
Editor:	**Ann Gosch**
Production Editor:	**Genevieve McDermott**
Production Artists:	**Nicole Phillips, Rich Lehl, and Betty Hopkins**
Manufacturing:	**Julia Coffey**

Trademarks

Crisp Fifty-Minute Series is a trademark of Axzo Press.

Some of the product names and company names used in this book have been used for identification purposes only and may be trademarks or registered trademarks of their respective manufacturers and sellers.

Disclaimer

We reserve the right to revise this publication and make changes from time to time in its content without notice.

ISBN 10: 1-4188-6490-0
ISBN 13: 978-1-4188-6490-3
Library of Congress Catalog Card Number 2005932134
Printed in the United States of America
6 7 09 08

Learning Objectives for

COMMUNICATION SKILLS FOR LEADERS

The learning objectives for *Communication Skills for Leaders* are listed below. They have been developed to guide the user to the core issues covered in this book.

The objectives of this book are to help the user:

1) Understand the importance of interpersonal communication skills to becoming a leader

2) Convey believability by ensuring the verbal, vocal, and visual elements of their communications deliver a consistent message

3) Replace negative or neutral habits with those that will improve their interpersonal effectiveness

4) Develop and practice the nine behavioral skills of effective interpersonal communication

5) Master the six skills of leadership

Assessing Progress

A Crisp Series **assessment** is available for this book. The 25-item, multiple-choice and true/false questionnaire allows the reader to evaluate his or her comprehension of the subject matter.

To download the assessment and answer key, go to www.courseilt.com and search on the book title.

Assessments should not be used in any employee-selection process.

About the Author

Bert Decker is a nationally recognized communications expert. The company he founded, Decker Communications, Inc., has been recognized for more than 20 years as one of the leading communications training companies.

Decker Communications provides communications consulting and skill building to more than 400 major organizations. The Decker Method™ is recognized as the best in its field for enhancing communication performance.

Bert Decker has also written the groundbreaking book, *You've Got To Be Believed To Be Heard,* and has appeared on the NBC Today show several times as its communications expert, commenting on the U.S. presidential debates.

Communication Skills for Leaders is based on the Decker Method™ and may be used effectively with the popular book *Creating Messages That Motivate* on the Decker Grid™, available through Decker Communications and at www.deckercommunications.com. Decker Communications, Inc. is headquartered at 104 Point Lobos, San Francisco, CA 94121, (415) 752-0700.

Preface

> Christine Figari is a trainer who has been with Decker Communications for more than 18 years. She first called me on the telephone when the company was only a couple years old and quite a bit leaner than it is today. "We're really not hiring new trainers right now," I said, "but go ahead and send your resume. We're always looking for good people."
>
> I was working in my office the next day when my receptionist, Bobbie, brought in Christine's resume and said, "I told her you wouldn't be able to talk to her without an appointment, but she insists on seeing you in person."
>
> I scanned the resume and saw that it was good, but not spectacular. I thought this was a little pushy, but figured I ought to at least be friendly, so I walked down the hall. I found Christine to be much more impressive than her resume.
>
> What really struck me was her certainty—energetic voice and manner, great posture, an authentic smile. She radiated confidence and competence. I learned more of what I needed to know about Chris within the first 30 seconds after we shook hands than from her entire resume.
>
> We ended up talking for half an hour. Two months later, I hired her.

The point of this story is that your personal impact *does* make a difference. Effective communication is critical in work and at play. It is particularly important to your professional effectiveness because of today's increasingly competitive environment.

Communication Skills for Leaders is an update of my previous edition, *The Art of Communicating*. This new edition explains the communication-leadership connection and includes updated examples to guide you in learning effective communication techniques.

Achieving excellence in interpersonal communications is a complex process made up of nine basic skills, which are presented in this book. You will learn why each is important and will be able to practice the skills through a variety of exercises, assessments, checklists, and self-tests. You will find yourself using your newfound skills dozens of times a day—both in business and your personal life.

Many of the ideas are commonsense. Some are new. Most important, they all work. They have been tested and proven by more than 300,000 business executives, managers, and salespeople who have participated in the Decker Method of Effective Communicating™ training programs.

Communicating is a learnable skill. It takes work, but the results are worth it. With practice you can raise this skill to an art form, and even enjoy the process.

Good luck!

Bert Decker

Bert Decker

The Communication-Leadership Connection

When we look for leaders, we look for people we *want* to lead us. And we tend to judge this "want" factor not so much from the information we have about the leaders, or from their credentials, or from race or intellect. No, the overwhelming factor that makes us want to follow certain leaders is their *ability to communicate effectively*—very effectively. These leaders know the art of communicating.

More Art Than Science

Communicating with another person is not a science. There is not a regimented set of precise and exacting procedures. There are specific, sound principles and themes, and thousands of variations on those themes. It is an art to use your skills and capabilities to best advantage within the framework of the principles outlined in this book.

Before Renoir, Monet, and Cezanne became master artists, they first became skilled and expert in basic brush strokes. They learned the principles of painting. Only then were they free to create masterpieces.

This book was designed to give you the "brush strokes" of interpersonal communications so that you, too, can create a masterpiece during your personal communications with others.

Interpersonal Communication in Daily Life

The emphasis in this book is on one-on-one communication in daily situations in which we exert "personal impact" (or lack of it). The principles, techniques, and skills in this book apply equally well to formal presentations or informal ones where people are continually judging our convictions and abilities.

In truth, we are all public speakers. The only "private speaking" that really goes on is in the privacy of our minds where our ideas bounce back and forth like ping-pong balls. This book refers to the "presentations" we give daily, when we present ourselves and our ideas to others.

Examples of where interpersonal communication skills are required include:

➢ **Within an Organization**

Interviews, meetings, coffee breaks, staff meetings, telephoning, performance reviews, company meetings, hallway conversations, working together on a project, job interviews, lunch breaks, project reviews, negotiating a raise.

➢ **With Customers or the Public**

Customer service, selling, telemarketing, reception desk, association meetings and conventions, TV appearances, telephone press interviews, in-person press interviews, telephoning, promoting, negotiating.

➢ **In Personal Life**

Family meetings, church groups, PTA, parties, telephoning, sports events, dinner parties, parent-child discussions, counseling sessions, wedding proposals.

What other situations can you think of that require effective interpersonal communication skills? List them here:

_____

_____

_____

As you can see, interpersonal communications are not confined to any single aspect of our lives. We communicate interpersonally every time we interact with others. The opportunities for interpersonal communications are almost limitless.

How effectively we communicate interpersonally ultimately determines how successful we become.

Developing Interpersonal Communication Skills

Some people seem to be born with a natural energy and confidence. Others must work at it. Consider the story of one shy and introspective college sophomore:

> His professor said he would not amount to much unless he projected himself more forcefully. This hurt a lot because the young man came from a family of leaders.
>
> The professor's remark changed the young man's life because he immediately embarked on an energetic self-improvement program. The college sophomore's name was Norman Vincent Peale.

For all of us, the qualities of those who lead and succeed can be learned and strengthened. All it takes is a conscious effort to learn and apply personal communication skills on a consistent basis with the help of some honest feedback.

This is what this book is all about. Let's get started.

Table of Contents

Appendix   89

Keys to Effective Interpersonal Communication

The Significance of Believability

The ability to express an idea is well nigh as important as the idea itself."

— **Bernard Baruch**

Most of us would agree that in business, as in all of life, the success of any presentation depends on the *believability* of the person speaking. Indeed, a person's believability is critical to any interpersonal success. No matter what is said, it is not going to make much difference to the listener unless the speaker is credible and believed. There can be no action where there is not belief and agreement.

This is not news to most people. What *is* news is that this is not normally taught in our schools. Even more important, it is not generally the way we conduct our interpersonal communications in business.

"Selling" Ourselves Through Communication

The most critical of all communication is face-to-face—when we are communicating about our ideas, ourselves, or our products. At the same time, we are also "selling" our ideas, ourselves, and our products. For example:

> ➤ The owner of a new business must be able to effectively sell a business plan to obtain financing or credit.

> ➤ A supervisor must be able to clearly communicate the goals of the organization to employees.

> ➤ A manager must be able to confront an employee who may also be a friend when there is poor performance.

> ➤ A parent must be confident enough to speak up at a school board meeting when pushing for a change.

> ➤ An executive in a difficult situation must be calm and confident enough to communicate the facts believably.

This book reflects the practical application of the latest research along with extensive observation about what really counts during successful communications. It applies to public speaking as well as to the dozens of informal presentations we give daily. Interpersonal communication skill is the ability to continually build credibility and believability into everything we communicate.

Verbal, Vocal, Visual Cues to Believability

Three elements are communicated each time we speak—verbal, vocal, and visual. The verbal is the message itself—the words the speaker says. The vocal element is the voice—intonation, projection, and resonance of the voice that carries those words. And the visual element is what listeners see—primarily the speaker's face and body.

UCLA Professor Albert Mehrabian, one of the foremost experts in personal communications, conducted a landmark study on the relationships among these three elements. He measured the differences in believability among the verbal, vocal, and visual elements. What his research found was that the degree of consistency among these three elements is what determines believability.

In the spaces provided, write your estimate of how much believability each of these elements conveys when you are speaking (interpersonal communication) to persuade a listener. The percentages should total 100.

Verbal	_____	%
Vocal	_____	%
Visual	_____	%
Total	**100**	**%**

Now turn to the next page for the results of Mehrabian's research.

Consistency = Believability

Professor Mehrabian's communications research, reported in his book *Silent Messages*, was based on what observers believed when an individual's verbal, vocal, and visual elements conveyed messages *inconsistent* with one another. When Mehrabian tested inconsistent messages, he found that the verbal cues were dominant only 7% of the time, the vocal 38% of the time, and the visual cues were the primary carrier of trust and believability, a whopping 55% of the time.

Verbal	7	%
Vocal	38	%
Visual	55	%
Total	**100**	**%**

If the message is *consistent,* then all three elements work together. The excitement and enthusiasm of the voice work with the energy and animation of the face and body to reflect the confidence and conviction of what is said. The words, the voice, and the delivery are all of a piece and the message gets through.

But when we are nervous or awkward or under pressure, we tend to block our content and give an inconsistent message. For example, if you look downward, clasp your hands in front of you in an inhibiting fig-leaf position, and speak in a halting and tremulous voice as you say "I am excited to be here"—you are delivering an inconsistent message. The words will not be believed.

Deliver Your Payload

When you are presenting your idea, you want to deliver your message into the heart and mind of every listener. Compare that with a rocket delivery system. There is the payload, or rocket ship, which a large Atlas or Titan booster rocket must launch into orbit. Without a strong, powerful booster rocket, it does not matter how well crafted the payload is because it will never get there.

In communication, your message is the payload. If you are nervous or wooden, your delivery system will go awry and your payload will not be delivered.

Some people in business are like a cannon ready to fire. They are a rocket with no payload. They may have great delivery skills but no verbal content. Others have detailed, brilliant ideas and productive things to say—technical and financial information—but they block the delivery system to get it out there.

A large majority of people in business give inconsistent messages. This inconsistency is probably the biggest barrier to effective interpersonal communications in business.

Making the Emotional Connection

Another barrier to effective interpersonal communication is not reaching listeners' unconscious, *feeling* level. Extensive research has dramatized the importance of making this emotional connection. Indeed, it is a widely accepted principle of marketing and sales that people "buy on emotion and justify with fact."

Whether what you are "selling" are widgets or yourself and your ideas, whether your listener is one person or one thousand, if you do not connect with your listeners' emotions, you will not connect with them very effectively.

This is because of our two distinct brains—the *first brain* and the *new brain*. The first brain is our emotional brain, which physically, and often unconsciously, directs our thinking brain, or what could be called the new brain.

Understanding the Two Brains

The first brain consists of the emotionally powerful limbic system, which is the emotional center, and the brain stem, which provides immediate instinctual response. The first brain is primitive, primal, and powerful. It operates at the unconscious level.

The largest part of the brain, the cerebrum, consists of a very thin layer of brain cells called the cerebral cortex. All conscious thought, including language and decision-making, takes place within this thin layer of brain cells—the new brain.

All sensory input—sight, sound, touch, taste, and smell—goes through the first brain first. The visual input from our eyes goes directly to the first brain. Then it gets forwarded to the thinking new brain, which makes sense of it, or interprets it. If the visual pathways are not stimulated very much (no movement, eye contact, gestures, etc.), the information does not get passed on as readily by the first brain to the new brain.

The same happens with the sound of a voice. The audio signals go into the first brain before being transferred to the new brain. If the sound tends to be flat, monotone, or filled with distracting nonwords, the first brain will tend to shut down and filter the information that is passed on.

The first brain is a lookout, a defense mechanism, a channel for communications that provides positive sensory input. The first brain also controls and triggers other emotions, such as distrust, anxiety, and indifference because of what it sees and hears unconsciously. The first brain is your mind's gatekeeper. It is this primitive part of the brain that gives intuitive impressions.

Have you ever met someone you immediately disliked? That is your first brain reacting instinctively to a warning or signal that you might not even be aware of. Have you experienced love at first sight? Again, this is the first brain in action, making a quick, intuitive judgment.

It is the first brain that decides what information to let into the more developed and reasoning new brain. This is why you must make an emotional connection to be heard.

Comparing the First Brain and the New Brain

First Brain	New Brain
Instinctual and primitive	Intellectual and advanced
300 to 500 million years old	3 to 4 million years old
Emotional	Rational
Preconscious/Unconscious	Conscious
Source of instinctive survival responses: hunger, thirst, danger, sex, and parental care	Source of thought, memory, language, creativity, planning, and decision-making
Common to many animals	Uniquely human

Believing What We Like

Whether our first brain registers instant "like" or "dislike" of a person we encounter, there can be little doubt that what it is responding to is something that person is communicating—verbally, vocally, or visually. No wonder likeability is a major component of trust. If we respond positively to people's communication, we tend to like them, and research shows we tend to trust people we like. Likeability and believability are intertwined—and both are dependent on effective interpersonal communication.

Measuring the Personality Factor

The Gallup Poll has conducted a revealing communications poll for all of the U.S. presidential races starting with the Kennedy/Nixon contest in 1960—12 races in all. This poll is conducted just two months before the presidential election. It asks for voters' preference in three areas—issues, party affiliation, and likeability, or "the personality factor."

What the polls have found is that the personality factor, scientifically measured by the Staples Scalometer, has been the only consistent predictor of the outcome of every one of the presidential races.

The Stanford Study

Professor Thomas W. Harrell of the Stanford Graduate School of Business completed a 20-year study[1] relating to career success. Although there were no "certain passports to success," Harrell found there were three consistent personal qualities that appeared to have a positive effect on the careers of those studied. These included:

> ➤ An outgoing, ascendant personality

> ➤ A desire to persuade, talk, and work with people

> ➤ A need for power

Although interpersonal communication skills are not necessarily related to the third characteristic, they are certainly intertwined in the first two. This is the same personality factor described above.

These studies and polls show that personality plays a major role in the effectiveness of your interpersonal relationships. Whatever you strive for, you can be sure that communication is the skill that will get you there. Luckily, despite what you may have read, you can alter your personality and change your communication habits to help you improve your interpersonal skills.

---

[1] Stanford University Study: Harrell & Alpert, March 1986

Choosing Positive Communication Habits

Behavioral Skills for Interpersonal Effectiveness

Vocal delivery and the visual elements, as well as personality, likeability, and openness are the primary ingredients of high-level interpersonal communications. But what specific behavioral characteristics and traits make up these important ingredients?

The nine behavioral skills are:

1. Eye Communication

2. Posture and Movement

3. Gestures and Facial Expressions

4. Dress and Appearance

5. Voice and Vocal Variety

6. Language, Nonwords, and Pauses

7. Listener Involvement

8. Humor

9. The Natural Self

Hundreds of stimuli go into each behavioral skill area. These are subtle refinements in the listener's perception. But of these hundreds, there are only about half a dozen key elements for each of the nine skill areas. Improving your interpersonal communication skills comes from making these key elements into behaviors you practice habitually.

This part looks at habits and how we can work to replace less effective habits with those that will help improve our interpersonal communications.

Understanding Habitual Behaviors

All behaviors come from habits, and all of us have hundreds of interpersonal communication habits. Some of these are positive but some of them are negative. And all habits can be changed.

Think about the following habits you have. Those described below are harmless but ingrained:

➤ Fold your arms. Now do it the opposite way. Notice that when you fold your arms you automatically had one way to do it. When you tried the opposite way it seemed strange and uncomfortable.

➤ Clasp your hands together, putting one thumb over the other. Now reverse the process. You will find that one way was more comfortable for you. (The greater comfort of one thumb or the other is seldom related to left-handedness or right-handedness.)

➤ Do you always brush your teeth in the morning, or at night? Do you have the same order when you wash your hands or face or take a shower?

➤ Do you always take the same route or transportation to work, or do you vary the route?

➤ Think of your eating habits: whether you have milk, water, or wine with a meal; whether you eat your vegetables, meat, or potatoes first; whether you eat fast or slowly; what you eat; what restaurants you go to regularly; and when you go to the same restaurant whether you eat the same things.

➤ Now think of a habit of yours that you do not like. Usually such habits are a pleasure—but we overdo them. Eating too much. Drinking too much. Smoking. Never getting angry, or getting angry too much. Most of us have areas of our life that are just … too much. Take a look.

All of these habits are not necessarily good or bad, but they are habits. And because they are habits, *you seem to have no choice about how you do them at the conscious level.*

The point is not to analyze which way you fold your arms or eat a meal. These things are not important, so it does not make much sense to change these habits. But there are habits that are worth working on.

In interpersonal communications, some habits will either enhance or detract from your effectiveness. These are the ones to concentrate on.

Changing Your Habits

To change any habit takes practice—framing, forming, and molding the mind to do certain physical behaviors that are repeated over and over. In his book *Psycho-Cybernetics,* Maxwell Maltz wrote that it takes 21 days to change a habit. Other studies have verified this.

The problem is that habits can seem like a huge elephant on our backs. The only way to cut that elephant down to size is to whittle it down to "bite-size" pieces. It is the same with our habits. To change them takes practice in bite-size pieces.

Start Small

To sensitize yourself to your habits and increase your habit-changing skills, start small and practice by following these tips:

➤ Choose simple, little everyday habits you may want to change (for example, to read for pleasure at least 15 minutes every day).

➤ Change three habits. Take one morning habit, one afternoon habit, and one evening habit for starters. Make it a campaign to work on them every day, no matter what.

➤ Look at the different areas of your life for your habit changes, such as eating habits, sleeping habits, coffee break habits, recreation habits, sexual habits, dressing habits, or work habits.

As creatures of habit, we do not easily change, so do not give up if you cannot change your habits overnight.

The next few pages cover Abraham Maslow's Four Steps of Learning and how they are related to the Four Stages of Speaking. This information will allow you to evaluate and rank which of your interpersonal habits need work and will give you some guidelines for making positive improvements in your interpersonal effectiveness.

The Four Stages of Learning

Maslow provides a valuable conceptual framework to understand how we learn anything. As we work through the stages, we advance from a lack of awareness of what we don't know to knowing something so well that we don't even have to think about it.

Stage 1: Unconscious Incompetence—We don't know that we don't know.

An energetic two-year-old boy wants to ride a bike that he sees his older brother riding. But he does not know that he doesn't know how to ride it. All he says is, "Mommy, I want to ride the bike." Most of us in business who have never had extensive feedback about our interpersonal skills are at this state of unconscious incompetence. We simply are not aware of our interpersonal communication habits.

Stage 2: Conscious Incompetence—We know that we don't know.

At this stage we learn that we are not competent at something. This often comes as a rude awakening. The two-year-old boy gets on a bike and falls off. He has immediately gone from stage one to stage two and knows that he does not know how to ride a bike. The same thing happens with a communicator when he finds out for the first time that he has a distracting habit, such as the "slow blink" or the "fig leaf" gesture.

Stage 3: Conscious Competence—We work at what we don't know.

Here we consciously make an effort to learn a new skill. Practice, drill, and repetition are at the forefront. This is where most learning takes place. It takes effort and work. The little boy carefully steers and balances and pedals and thinks of what he is doing, step by step. The person with a slow blink (or a fig leaf or other distracting habit) consciously works at changing the habit.

Stage 4: Unconscious Competence—We don't have to think about knowing it.

Here the skill takes over automatically at an unconscious level. The little boy rides his bike without even thinking about it. He can whistle, talk, sing, or engage his mind in other things at the same time. A speaker with a distracting habit who has learned to overcome it through practice does not have to concentrate on not doing the distracting habit.

The Four Stages of Speaking

The four stages of speaking are related to the four stages of learning, although they are not parallel. All communicators are in one of the four stages of speaking. To advance from one to the next requires going through the four stages of learning.

Stage 1: The Nonspeaker

People at this level avoid "public" speaking at all costs. Their mind-set is one of terror. These people will go to great lengths not to speak formally. They sometimes get trapped, but in general are adept at finding excuses (like illness) so they won't have to present themselves or their ideas publicly. Their interpersonal communication skills tend to be low, and they generally work in jobs that do not require speaking skills.

Stage 2: The Occasional Speaker

People at this level reluctantly accept speaking assignments. They almost never volunteer. They recognize, however, that they must be able to present their ideas if they want to get ahead. They will speak when necessary. Their fear is inhibiting, but not debilitating. This is the easiest stage to advance from—just by practicing the act of speaking.

Stage 3: The Willing Speaker

Fear is not a drawback at this level. The mind-set is one of tension. These speakers have learned to use emotions positively. They will speak their mind in business meetings. In general they are willing to put themselves out front—although they sometimes need a little nudge—and they know they will do well. But they still have some trepidation.

Stage 4: The Leader

Speaking stimulates these folks. They are driven to present themselves and their ideas—they know the rewards to be reaped. Leaders "speak for a living" by motivating people and speaking up and out in all situations. They can inspire and their roles in business are, by definition, as leaders.

Using Video Feedback to Change Personal Perceptions

As can be seen from the four stages of learning, awareness of habits is critical to any behavior change. Feedback is what enables this awareness, which is why feedback is so important to creating change. In interpersonal communications, video feedback is especially effective.

Our effectiveness in interpersonal communications is directly related to our confidence level. It is valuable, therefore, to use video feedback for an objective look at how we come across to others. People often find out they are better than they thought they were.

San Francisco State University sponsored a study that documents such changes in perception.[1] A statistically valid survey was done with 2,000 participants in an intensive two-day video feedback program. They placed themselves in four stages of speaking *before* having video feedback and then again *after* seeing themselves in different communicating circumstances during the two-day period. Following are the results:

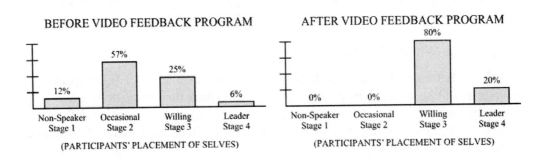

BEFORE VIDEO FEEDBACK PROGRAM

57%

25%

12%

6%

| Non-Speaker Stage 1 | Occasional Stage 2 | Willing Stage 3 | Leader Stage 4 |

(PARTICIPANTS' PLACEMENT OF SELVES)

AFTER VIDEO FEEDBACK PROGRAM

80%

20%

0%   0%

| Non-Speaker Stage 1 | Occasional Stage 2 | Willing Stage 3 | Leader Stage 4 |

(PARTICIPANTS' PLACEMENT OF SELVES)

As you can see from the graphs, once people had the opportunity to see themselves on video, they realized their speaking ability was better than they thought. This elevated their perceptions of themselves, enabling them to feel more willing to speak up.

Likewise, if, through feedback, you are able to elevate your perception of your interpersonal communication skills, you are more likely to make the most of your strengths and work to improve on your weak areas.

[1] San Francisco State University College of Business Study, 1985

Developing the Nine Behavioral Skills

Behavioral Skill #1: Eye Communication

> ❝ *An eye can threaten like a loaded and leveled gun; or can insult like hissing and kicking; or in its altered mood, by beams of kindness, make the heart dance with joy.*❞
>
> **–Ralph Waldo Emerson**

Eye communication is the most important skill in your personal impact toolbox. Your eyes are the only part of your central nervous system that directly connects with another person. Do not assume that simply making "eye contact" is enough. Good eye communication means more than just a fleeting glance.

Behavioral Objective

Your goal in developing your eye communication skills is to *look sincerely and steadily at another person*.

In individual communications, normal eye communication should be from five to 15 seconds. To individuals in a group, it should be four to five seconds. Make this a habit so that when you are under pressure you will maintain a confident eye pattern, without the need to think about it.

Aiming for Involvement with Your Listener

The "three I's" of eye communication are intimacy, intimidation, and involvement. Intimacy and intimidation mean looking at another person for a long period—from 10 seconds to a minute or more. But more than 90% of our personal communications (especially in business settings) call for *involvement.* This is the basis of this section.

➤ **Five Seconds for More Effectiveness**

When we talk to others and are excited, enthusiastic, and confident, we usually look at them for five to 10 seconds before looking away. This is natural in a one-on-one communication. It is also what you should strive for in all situations—whether speaking to one person or one thousand. This five-second period is what listeners are comfortable with in the majority of their communications.

➤ **Beware of the Eye Dart**

What most of us tend to do when we feel pressure is to glance at anything but our listener. Our eyes tend to dart every which way like those of a scared rabbit. This conveys nervousness, which undermines our credibility. Anything other than looking directly at the person we are talking to increases the tendency toward darting eyes and makes our listener uncomfortable.

➤ **Beware of the Slow Blink**

As disconcerting as the eye dart is the slow blink, in which you might keep your eyelids closed for up to two or three seconds. It conveys the message, "I really don't want to be here." Usually, your listeners will not want to be either.

➤ **Speaking to Large Groups**

If you are addressing a large group, then extended eye communication (five seconds) is particularly important. In a large group, audience members in close proximity to an individual you are actually looking at will sense that you are looking at them. The farther back the individuals, the more people who will feel included in your gaze. As a result, you can "cover" many audience members in one five-second gaze before shifting your eye contact to another section of the group.

➤ **Eye Communication and Television**

When you are being interviewed on video or television (such as a training video or even home videotape), it is important to have good, steady eye communication with the interviewer and any others whom the camera can see. Never look directly at the camera. The TV audience is observing you through the means of the camera, so treat the camera as the "observer" it really is.

Eye Communication Patterns in Business

You use your eyes to communicate 90% of the time in business (excluding the telephone). As you communicate with colleagues, customers, managers, and other business associates, concentrate on how you look at them. Envision how you look when you are upset or are pleased. As a salesperson, focus on how you look at tough clients before a sale. Compare that to how you look when you have just closed a sale.

Notice the eye patterns of others during job interviews and performance appraisals. Then take your newfound awareness and apply it to more effective and confident eye patterns of your own.

Examples of Eye Communication

➤ Kathy is a manager of the IT department. When she talks to people, she tends to keep her eyes closed two to three seconds between glances, causing perhaps a calm stance, but giving the impression of aloofness, shyness, or some other form of not caring. This habit pattern also carries into her formal presentations. She does not know she has "slow blink," which causes her listeners to feel distance.

➤ John is a film producer who habitually looks at the lower right cheek of his listeners. He gives an impression of awkwardness and distance without knowing it.

➤ Maria is personnel director for a major corporation. As she interviews people, she often looks out her window as she talks and asks questions, appearing uninterested and distant.

➤ As a professional speaker, Pat excites audiences with dramatic personal stories and anecdotes—except that she undermines her personal impact by looking at people in her audience for about half a second, or less. Pat believes she has good eye contact, but the individuals in her audience do not feel she is talking right to them.

IMPROVING YOUR EYE COMMUNICATION

Listed below are skill development exercises and tips to extend your eye communications in the dozens of interpersonal communications you have daily. Practice each of these daily. At first, these practices may feel awkward or embarrassing; but as with other learned behaviors, regular practice will increase your confidence, and your eye communication will show steady improvement.

1. Where Do You Look?

In your next 10 conversations, determine where you generally look when you talk to others. Note that you do not look directly in both eyes. You may look either at a person's left eye or right eye, but it is impossible to look at both at the same time. In one-on-one conversations, our eyes tend to move around the face, but there is one predominant place most of us tend to rest. Find where your spot is—the right eye? bridge of the nose? left eye? directly between the eyes? Any resting place near the eyes is acceptable. Not acceptable is anywhere else (the floor, over your listener's shoulder, etc.).

Once you have found your pattern, increase your awareness and sensitize yourself to the complexities of eye communication. Then try to look somewhere else and feel the dissonance. This will help desensitize you to feelings of awkwardness when you might not want to look directly at someone, but should for effectiveness.

2. Reinforce the Five-Second Habit

When you are in a meeting or giving a speech, ask a friend to count how long you look at specific individuals. Consciously keep five-second eye communication with individuals in the group to whom you are communicating.

3. Increase Sensitivity

Talk to a partner for about a minute. Ask him to look away from you after 15 seconds as you continue talking. For the rest of the exercise have him look anywhere else but at you while he is still listening. How does this feel? Reverse this process and then discuss the relevance of eye communication in verbal conversations. Then notice how often good eye contact is lacking at certain social functions (such as parties). Practice better eye contact in these informal situations and realize what a difference it makes to a conversation.

CONTINUED

CONTINUED

4. Relieve Intimidation

If you feel uncomfortable with an individual you must talk to (such as in a job interview or a meeting with the company president), try looking at that person's forehead. To experiment with this, get in a conversation with a partner sitting four or five feet away. Look at the middle of her forehead, just above her eyes. She will think you have good eye communication with her. But you will not feel as if you are "in touch" at all. This will help reduce the emotional connection so it is almost like talking to a wall. Reverse the process so your partner can experience the same phenomenon.

5. Analyze Eye Communication in Yourself and Others

Observe others (either in person or on TV) and notice how different an individual's eye communication patterns make you feel about the person. Videotape yourself so you can see your eye patterns. Ask friends how they feel about your eye communication. Ask a friend or associate to analyze your eye contact in various communication circumstances.

PERSONAL GOAL WORKSHEET

Determine your answer for each question below and place a check (✓) in the appropriate box. You may not yet know your own communication skills well enough to answer every question, but review the book regularly until you can.

Yes	*No*	
_____	_____	Do you know where you look when you are talking to another person?
_____	_____	Are you aware where you look when you are listening to another person?
_____	_____	Do you have a feel for how long to maintain eye communication in a one-on-one conversation?
_____	_____	Do you know how long to maintain eye communication with specific individuals when presenting to a large group?
_____	_____	Are you aware where you look when you look away from a person?
_____	_____	Do you know whether you have "eye dart" or "slow blink"?
_____	_____	Do you realize that eye communication is the most important behavioral skill in interpersonal communications?

CONTINUED

Now write down three of your habitual patterns in eye communication that you may want to modify, strengthen, or eliminate:

1. _____

   _____

2. _____

   _____

3. _____

   _____

Then write what you plan to practice to modify, strengthen, or change each habit.

1. _____

   _____

2. _____

   _____

3. _____

   _____

Remember: Practice Makes Permanent

Behavioral Skill #2: Posture and Movement

> *Stand tall. The difference between towering and cowering is totally a matter of inner posture. It's got nothing to do with height, it costs nothing, and it's more fun."*
>
> **–Malcolm Forbes**

Think of a public figure you often see on TV—a newscaster, politician, celebrity, pundit. Can you think of any who are "slumpers"? Probably not many, since confidence is usually expressed through excellent posture.

How you hold yourself physically can reflect how you hold yourself psychologically. And how you hold yourself is usually how others regard you. People tend to treat you as you "ask" to be treated.

Behavioral Objective

Your goal in developing your posture and movement skills is to *stand tall and move naturally and easily*.

You must correct the general tendency to slump in both upper and lower body posture. When communicating, it is more effective to be fluid rather than locked into rigid positions. This applies to all gestures, but particularly to leg and foot movements.

Examples: Posture and Movement

➤ Felicia runs her own consulting firm. As a little girl, she thought she had a big tummy, so she consciously sucked in her stomach and stood up straight with her shoulders back. Now as an adult she has very erect body posture, which conveys confidence. As a result, she commands attention when she enters a room.

➤ Eric works in a television studio. He grew so fast that in eighth grade he was six feet, two inches tall. He tried to diminish his height by slumping. Now as an adult, he is a stoop-shouldered six-foot-six. Although he now has the self-esteem he lacked as a youngster, his early posture habit causes him to appear hesitant and lacking in confidence.

➤ Alberto is president of a major transportation company. When he makes a formal presentation, he stands behind the lectern, hands nervously gripping the sides. He is chained to the spot, looking more like an employee than a president. After taking a communications course, he began moving out from behind the lectern and felt himself free and natural, rather than anchored to one spot. He had all his employees go through the communication course.

➤ Delisa was 17 when she volunteered to participate in a videotape demonstration during a communications seminar. She was to talk for a few minutes, then during the next week participate in the seminar before returning to speak on camera again. This was a "before and after" experiment. Although several things were different, most remarkable was her posture change. When she first talked, she leaned on her left hip and was casually stooped. The next week the TV audience first saw her as she strode from behind the curtain and stood tall. Even before she opened her mouth, she exuded a confidence that was almost tangible.

Keys to Effective Posture and Movement

There is no absolute right or wrong way to stand or move. But there are concepts that work, and these are outlined in this section. Be sure to adapt posture and movement concepts to your personal style.

➢ **Stand Tall**

Poor upper body posture often reflects low self-esteem. At least this is how other people see it, until they have enough other information to change this opinion. Many times upper body posture comes from an outdated habit pattern. Many tall men walk around hunched over because they grew fast as adolescents and did not want to stand out. Others simply never considered posture to be important and allowed the slouching and slumping teenage period to extend into adulthood.

➢ **Watch Your Lower Body**

The second part of posture that often gets neglected is the lower body. When you are talking to others, you may decrease your effectiveness because of the way you stand. You can divert your communication energy away from your listeners through inappropriate body language. One of the most common adverse posture patterns is going back on one hip. If you tend to do this, you are subconsciously saying, "I don't want to be here." You are literally distancing yourself from others. Other variations are rocking from side to side, going back and forth on your heels and toes, or pacing.

➢ **Use the "Ready Position"**

What you can do to combat these negative habits is to take the "ready position," or weight forward. Communication rides on a "horse" of energy. When you are speaking—when you are confident and want to get your message across—you have your energy forward. The ready position is leaning slightly forward so you could bounce up and down on the balls of your feet, with your knees slightly flexed. It is similar to practicing for athletic competition, in which you are ready to move in any direction. When your weight is forward, it is impossible to go back on one hip or rock back and forth on your heels. Get in the habit of the ready position in both formal and informal communication situations, and you'll be ready when the heat is on.

➢ **Move**

Communication and energy cannot be separated. Use all of your natural energy in a positive fashion. When you are speaking to others, move around. Come out from behind the lectern if you are in a formal situation. This will remove the physical barrier between yourself and others. In a group meeting, you have space to move a bit—your feet as well as your hands or arms. If you are seated, consider standing when you are "on" or leaning forward to give yourself more impact. Movement increases your energy, reflects confidence, and adds variety to your communications. Do not overdo it, but do move within your own natural energy level. Although high-energy people have an advantage, greater personal impact is available to all who stay conscious of using what they have.

IMPROVING YOUR POSTURE AND MOVEMENT

Listed below are several skill development exercises and tips for posture and movement in the dozens of interpersonal communications you have daily.

1. See Yourself

You can readily monitor your posture and movement through mirrors or others' observations. Better yet, if you can arrange it, videotape yourself walking and talking, and then observe the tape. Notice your upper body position—standing tall? hunching down? somewhere in between? If you cross your legs and lean against walls when you are standing informally, you will notice that it often appears sloppy rather than casual. Try variations of the ready position to see how that looks.

2. Walk Away from the Wall

The upper body posture of beauty pageant contestants is erect and confident. One reason is the "walk away from the wall" exercise of Miss America 1964 Donna Axum. Stand against a wall with your heels and shoulders touching the wall. Then straighten your spine so that the small of your back is also touching the wall. Walk away from the wall (shake a little so you are not rigid) and then walk a few steps. Notice how you feel tall and project more confidence. If you practice this regularly, you can improve your posture dramatically.

3. Do the "Two-Step"

The next time you are talking to a group, have someone count the number of steps you take (if you move at all). Often we take tentative half-steps because we want to move but feel inhibited. That degree of movement is better than none, but still reflects exactly what we feel—tentativeness. If you do the "two-step" instead, taking at least two steps toward someone, you will force yourself to move with apparent purpose. When you combine that with good eye communication, you will be talking and presenting yourself in a confident, direct fashion.

4. Stand at Meetings

Experiment with posture and movement. At your next meeting, stand when you have something important to say. This will give your message more emphasis. When you go into a one-on-one meeting to sell a product or an idea, consider making a stand-up presentation, perhaps even using a visual aid such as a flip chart.

PERSONAL GOAL WORKSHEET

Determine your answer for each question below and place a check (✓) in the appropriate box. You may not yet know your own communication skills well enough to answer every question, but review the book regularly until you can.

Yes   *No*

_____ _____ Do you lean back on one hip when you are talking in a small group?

_____ _____ Do you cross your legs when you are standing and chatting informally?

_____ _____ Is your upper body posture erect—shoulders in a straight line rather than curving inward toward your chest?

_____ _____ When you speak formally, do you plant yourself behind a lectern or table?

_____ _____ Do you communicate impatience by tapping your foot or a pencil when you are listening?

_____ _____ Do you know if you have the "fig leaf" pose or other nervous or inhibiting gestures when addressing a group?

_____ _____ Do you move around when talking informally?

CONTINUED

Now write down three of your habitual patterns of posture and movement that you may want to modify, strengthen, or eliminate:

1. _____

   _____

2. _____

   _____

3. _____

   _____

Then write what you plan to practice to modify, strengthen, or change each habit.

1. _____

   _____

2. _____

   _____

3. _____

   _____

Remember: Practice Makes Permanent

Behavioral Skill #3: Gestures and Facial Expressions

> *We don't 'know' our presidents. We imagine them. We watch them intermittently and from afar, inferring from only a relatively few gestures and reactions what kind of people they are and whether they should be in charge. Much depends on our intuition and their ability at a handful of opportune moments to project qualities we admire and respect."*
>
> **–Meg Greenfield**

Communication reflects energy. Those born with extra energy have an advantage. But we all can be aware of and increase our energy level. This is most apparent in our gestures and facial expressions.

Behavioral Objective

Your goal in developing your skills with gestures and facial expressions is *to be relaxed and natural when you speak.*

To be effective at interpersonal communication, you should have your hands and your arms relaxed and natural at your sides when you are at rest. You should gesture naturally when animated and enthusiastic. You should learn to smile under pressure, in the same way you would with a natural smile when you are comfortable.

Examples: Gestures and Facial Expressions

➤ Ted participated in a videotape seminar in which he gave a two-minute introduction. He started with his hands in the "fig leaf" position and then switched into something worse. With his hands in the fig-leaf position, he would raise his cupped hands every two seconds. When he saw it later on video playback, he called himself the "fig leaf flasher." He was so shocked at the distraction that he worked to change his habit and never "flashed" again.

➤ Charles rose through the ranks to become senior vice president of a major advertising agency. His employees thought he was always in a bad mood because his face looked grim and serious. He was also quizzical when his children would say, "What's wrong, Dad?" It was not until he did some experimenting in front of a video camera that he saw what others meant. Even when smiling on the inside, nothing showed through on the outside. Surprisingly, when he tried to exaggerate a smile, it didn't look exaggerated—it showed excitement and enthusiasm.

➤ In the 2004 U.S. presidential debates between President George Bush and Senator John Kerry, much was made of the two candidates' behavior when they were not speaking. There were smirks, frowns, and grimaces—so much so that in the debate commentary, more was said about the reaction shots than about the content of the dialogue. For subsequent debates, each candidate changed his facial expressions to be more neutral and natural while listening to the other, which silenced the spin doctors on this topic.

Keys to Effective Gestures and Facial Expressions

To communicate effectively, you need to be as open as possible in your face and gestures—*in a way that is natural for you*. You can work to ensure better gestures and facial expressions in the following ways:

➢ **Find Out Your Habits**

Find how you look to others when you are under pressure. Get this to the conscious level. You can make this discovery through feedback from others, but best of all, view and observe yourself on videotape. You have to know what you are doing that is not natural before you can be natural. You need to be able to recognize your habits at the level of conscious incompetence.

➢ **Find Your Nervous Gestures**

We all have gestures we tend to use when we are speaking without anything to hold onto. Find out what your primary gesture is and then do anything but that gesture. Do not try to gesture at certain words or phrases—it doesn't work well. Just concentrate on not doing your nervous gesture. Your hands should fall to your sides when you are not emphasizing an idea or point. When you do want the emphasis that comes from natural enthusiasm, it will occur naturally. But it cannot occur if your hands are stuck in your pockets or locked in a nervous gesture or if your arms are crossed.

➢ **You Can't Overexaggerate**

Very few people exaggerate their gestures or facial expressions. This is such a dramatic finding that it is almost possible to say that you cannot overexaggerate. Push yourself. Try to exaggerate your positive gestures. You would be surprised at how normal they actually look. Do not worry about overdoing it.

➢ **Smile—Which Third Are You In?**

We all think that we smile much of the time. In reality, others observe us as having a very strong predisposition to either smiling or not smiling. Studies have shown that about one-third of people in business have naturally open and smiling faces. Another third tend to have neutral faces that can readily go from a smile to a serious and intense look. And another one-third have faces that are serious and intense, whether they think they are smiling or not.

Find out which third you are in. Ask others to help you. If you are in the easily smiling third, you have a distinct advantage in your communications with others. People will perceive you as open and friendly and will be more open to your ideas. Another advantage is that you can also convey bad news more readily than others. If you are in the neutral third, easily moving from a smiling face to a serious one, you have flexibility. But if you are in the "solemn" one-third, you have to work on this area of your communications. You may be smiling on the inside, but your face may reflect doom and gloom on the outside. And that is exactly what you communicate. Perception is reality in the eyes of the beholder.

➤ **Remember the Personality Factor**

Your gestures, particularly your facial expressions, will tend to show you to be open and close, or closed and distant to those with whom you are communicating. Remember that people will buy your ideas and be persuaded much more readily if they like you. People like people who are more open. It pays to cultivate the personality factor. Serious people, such as technocrats, analysts, programmers, engineers, and academicians, can be effective in person, but they are usually more effective in writing. Interpersonal communication means connecting with another person on an *emotional* level, not just an intellectual level.

➤ **Smiles Have Muscles**

There is nothing mysterious about a smile, except the effect it has. It is physically caused by muscles and they can be exercised. Practicing smiling is not as much about moving your lips into a smile as it is about raising your cheekbones. Consider the upper part of your cheeks as apples and just lift your apples to smile. Put muscle into your smile.

➤ **Caution: Phony Smiles Do Not Work**

Smiling is such an important interpersonal skill because it immediately communicates how you are feeling—or at least people will perceive how you are feeling by the look on your face. So it is important to become aware of how you smile. But beware that phony smiles do not work. Not only do they not last, but they are perceived as phony. You want to train yourself to smile through practice with your facial muscles, but remember that a true smile comes from within. It is like practicing a sport and training your muscles so they are ready to use at the right time—when you are motivated by the adrenaline of competition.

Improving Your Gestures and Facial Expressions

Listed below are several skill development exercises and tips to enhance your gestures and facial expressions in the dozens of interpersonal communications you have daily.

1. **Practice Gesturing with a Partner/Observer**

   Stand six to eight feet from another person who will be your observer. Talk about how your hands and arms feel as they are resting at your sides. Then continue talking about gestures in general and how they feel when they are natural. Gesture normally as you speak. Then exaggerate your gestures, even moving a little bit if you feel like it, and describe to your partner how you are feeling as you do so. Make sure your gestures are exaggerated—and that they go above your waist and out to the side. Then ask your partner for feedback. Probably she will tell you that she did not feel that you exaggerated as much as you felt you did. Reverse the process and let your partner do the gesturing and you give the feedback. Practice this exercise several times until you get a good feel for how "energetic" you can be without being perceived as exaggerated.

2. **Count Your Nervous Gestures**

   The next time you speak in front of a group, have someone count the number of times you display your nervous gesture. This can be at a meeting or in a formal or informal speaking situation. If your nervous gesture is the "fig leaf," for example, tell this to your observer and then have him count the number of times during the presentation that you display the fig leaf. This will sensitize you to how serious your problem is and will be a good way to start modifying your behavior to do anything but your nervous gesture.

3. **Role-Playing**

   Look at a videotape or TV performance of a confident, forceful, energetic speaker. You might select a leader from politics, business, or athletics as your role model. Work through the following steps as you try to emulate that person:

   ➤ Take an actual presentation, preferably a business presentation, and deliver it to an individual or group in your usual manner. (This exercise is very effective in groups.)

   ➤ Then think about how your role model might deliver it.

➤ Put all of yourself into acting as if you are that person delivering your material. Remember, this is just a role-play and practice, so let it all hang out.

➤ Then ask for feedback from the group. (If possible, videotape both presentations so you will be able to see the difference in yourself.)

4. Go to an Electronics Store

Videotape feedback is extremely valuable for all behavioral skills, and particularly for gestures and facial expressions. Find a way to record yourself on videotape. If you have no other access, here is a way that can work for everybody. Go to your local electronics store and ask a salesperson to demonstrate a video camera. Have her tape you giving an impromptu talk of a minute or so and ask her to replay it. The following week go to another store and do the same thing. After several times, you will have experienced the value of video feedback. Then decide which system is best for you, and if you can afford a camera, buy one.

5. Watch Television with No Sound

Whether situation comedies, talk shows, or newscasts, take a look at television with the sound turned off. If you do this just five or 10 minutes a day, you will be amazed at how much is communicated by those you observe. Their interpersonal communications, believability, confidence, and credibility are largely conveyed through their gestures and facial expressions.

6. Test Your Smile

You can do this exercise alone if you have access to a video camera. Start the tape, look directly at the camera, and give a big phony smile. Describe to the camera how it feels to give that big phony smile. Spend 20 or 30 seconds with that big phony smile. Then, with the videotape continuing to run, wipe your face clean and convey what to you feels like a normal, easy, friendly smile. Describe how that feels on your face for 20 to 30 seconds. Then view your videotape.

If you are in the one-third of "nonsmilers," you may see that your phony smile does not look as bad as you thought and it at least conveys some degree of openness and friendliness. At the same time you may see that the natural smile you felt on the inside did not show at all on the outside. Often when you think you are smiling, you are actually looking serious.

PERSONAL GOAL WORKSHEET

Determine your answer for each question below and place a check (✓) in the appropriate box. You may not yet know your own communication skills well enough to answer every question, but review the book regularly until you can.

Yes   *No*

_____   _____   Are you aware whether you smile under pressure or become stone-faced?

_____   _____   When you talk on the phone, do you find yourself smiling rather than frowning?

_____   _____   Do you have an inhibiting gesture—an awkward place where your hands tend to go when speaking under pressure?

_____   _____   Do you ever raise your hand or arm above waist level when making a presentation to a group?

_____   _____   Do you lean forward and gesture when you are seated, just as you do when you are making a presentation?

_____   _____   Do you communicate impatience by drumming your fingers on the table when you are listening?

_____   _____   Do your fingers twitch if you try to keep them at your sides when you are speaking to a group?

CONTINUED

Now write down three of your habitual patterns in your use of gestures and facial expressions that you may want to modify, strengthen, or eliminate:

1. _____

_____

2. _____

_____

3. _____

_____

Then write what you plan to practice to modify, strengthen, or change each habit.

1. _____

_____

2. _____

_____

3. _____

_____

Remember: Practice Makes Permanent

Behavioral Skill #4:
Dress and Appearance

> 66 *You never get a second chance to make a good first impression."*

–John Molloy

The effect of your initial appearance on others is far greater than you may think. It is not a superficial thing, but communicates extensively to others how you feel about yourself. It also shows what you sometimes do just to get attention.

We form immediate and vivid impressions of people during the first three seconds we see them. Experts estimate that it takes another 30 seconds to add 50% more impression (negative or positive) to the impression we got in the first three seconds. If you take this concept further, you can calculate that it will take three minutes to add 50% more to the 30-second impression. So first impressions are very significant.

Behavioral Objective

Your goal in developing your skills with dress and appearance is to *look appropriate to the environment you are in, as well as for yourself.*

There is not so much a right or wrong way to dress or groom as an appropriate way. This means appropriate first of all in how comfortable *you* feel. This is more important than what others feel. If you feel uncomfortable, you will not communicate very effectively. Your appearance also should be appropriate to the company you are in, considering others' expectations, your geographical setting, the time of day, social situation, circumstances, and so on.

Keys to Effective Dress and Appearance

Because 90% of our body is covered by clothing, we need to be aware of what our clothes are communicating. (When we are uncovered, the same principle applies. Considering this, if we spend time at the beach or pool, we might be motivated to exercise a bit more.)

The 10% of the body not normally covered by clothes is largely the face and hair. This is the most important 10% of all because this is where people look. The impression others receive is very much influenced by how we groom our head—for example, hairstyle, makeup, and jewelry for women; hairstyle, facial hair, or lack of it for men.

Most of us dress based on past habits because we are creatures of habit. Take a careful and conscious look at how you dress and groom. Do you pick out a certain color because you always have? Does that color work for you? Do you wear certain shoes or eyeglasses because those are what you wore in college? Are they still *appropriate* today?

The following examples illustrate the importance of evaluating dress and appearance for the messages they convey.

Examples: Dress and Appearance

➤ A writer for *The New Yorker*, Malcolm Gladwell became a business phenomenon with his book *The Tipping Point*. Afterward he decided to let his hair grow from a closely cropped style into a full Afro. He found that people's reactions to him were significantly different from when he had short hair and that he was stopped on the highway by police officers more often. Why were police making incorrect snap judgments based on hairstyle, he wondered. These experiences led to his writing the influential book *Blink*, which explores the power of first impressions—those made, seemingly, "in the *blink* of an eye."

➤ A film producer for many years did business mostly in the sans-necktie "uniform" of a filmmaker. When speaking to business groups, he would concede to wear a tie and jacket. Today, more enlightened about dress and appearance, he is embarrassed to think of his audience's reaction the time he spoke to the 50 managers of a client company—while wearing a plaid sports jacket, vivid red shirt, and black knit tie.

IMPROVING YOUR DRESS AND APPEARANCE

Listed below are skill development exercises and tips to help you enhance your dress and appearance in the dozens of interpersonal communications you have daily.

1. The First Three Seconds

When you next meet a person for the first time, consciously keep a mental picture of how you *felt* about that person after the first impression. Then analyze how much came from dress, from expression, from hairstyle, from eye contact, from jewelry, and so on. What made a positive impression and what made a distracting impression? What was neutral? Do this exercise daily. It can also be a pleasant pastime at a party or social gathering.

2. Pick Five People

Write the names of five people you know well. Think of how you would *design* their dress and appearance differently. Pick it apart in detail—the clothes, shirts, skirts, ties, colors, patterns, makeup, hair, jewelry, glasses, and so on. It works best if you write out the changes so you will become *consciously* aware of the differences each of these elements make.

3. Nobody Will Tell You

Now that you have analyzed five other people, do the same for yourself. Analyze in detail what you do and what you should change. Realize that almost nobody will volunteer to tell you what needs changing. Dress and appearance is one of the most self-conscious and personally sensitive subjects in interpersonal communications, so few people will tell us what they really think and feel. You can help them provide feedback by just asking. It can help verify your own analysis.

4. Pick a New Outfit

Every day look at something in a new way. Choose one area, such as your shoes, dress, suit, jacket, tie, shirt, or grooming habit. Change it. Combine it with something to give a new look. Pick an appropriate but different outfit the next time you are shopping. Dressing differently daily will sensitize you to how you feel in your dress and appearance. It will also make you more aware of how others feel about your appearance. And it will help you discover what works well.

5. See a Consultant

Because dress and appearance have a great impact on how others perceive us, it is often worth the time and expense to consult a specialist. This can be a clothes consultant, color consultant, or makeup consultant. Be sure to check referrals because this is an area of "image intangibles" and you want to be sure you get good advice. You can consult specialized "shoppers" in department stores to assist in your clothes buying. Or seek assistance from online resources, such as www.firstimpressionmanagement.com.

6. Research, Research, Research

Read a book. John Molloy's books—*Dress for Success* in both men's and women's versions—are probably the best known. Although his opinions may not be to your taste, his research is extensive and the "rights and wrongs" according to Molloy are valuable to know. You can also find magazine and newspaper articles on the subject. Although they, too, are filled with subjective opinions, they will help increase your awareness. Then you can fit your own style and taste into the general principles.

7. Ask How You Look

The simplest way to get immediate feedback is to ask others, for example, "How does this look?" Although people will be sensitive to your feelings, if you are continually open and forthright, you will gain a valuable perspective on yourself. Do not be shy. Others will soon realize you are serious and will give you their honest opinions. If you act on the valid opinions you receive, your dress and appearance will become more and more effective.

PERSONAL GOAL WORKSHEET

Determine your answer for each question below and place a check (✓) in the appropriate box. You may not yet know your own communication skills well enough to answer every question, but review the book regularly until you can.

Yes   *No*

_____ _____ Have you tried wearing your hair a different way—parted on the other side, or frizzed, permed, crew-cut, sprayed, or tinted?

_____ _____ Do your glasses inhibit good eye communication?

_____ _____ Have you tried glasses vs. contact lenses? Is there a difference in effectiveness?

_____ _____ Do you organize the clothes in your closet by design?

_____ _____ Do people notice your jewelry?

_____ _____ Are people distracted by your jewelry?

_____ _____ Do you ever dress to shock people, or for effect, or for any reason other than to cover your body?

_____ _____ Are you always aware of your grooming? (For example, are your nails trimmed and clean? Do you bathe daily? Are your clothes always clean and pressed?)

CONTINUED

Now write down three of your habitual patterns in your dress and appearance that you may want to modify, strengthen, or eliminate:

1. _____

   _____

2. _____

   _____

3. _____

   _____

Then write what you plan to practice to modify, strengthen, or change each habit.

1. _____

   _____

2. _____

   _____

3. _____

   _____

Remember: Practice Makes Permanent

Behavioral Skill #5:
Voice and Vocal Variety

> " *The Devil hath not, in all his quiver's choice,*
> *An arrow for the heart like a sweet voice.* "

–Byron

Your voice is the primary vehicle to carry your message. It is like transportation—you can have an old jalopy that rattles along or a smooth-running, finely tuned automobile. Both will get you to your destination, but the quality of the ride can vary greatly.

Behavioral Objective

Your goal in developing your voice and vocal variety is to *use your voice as a rich, resonant instrument*, whether you are communicating with others in person, on the phone, or in a group setting. You want to command people's attention and not allow your voice to be a barrier to action.

Examples: Voice and Vocal Variety

➤ Alex is a well-known author who has written two nonfiction blockbusters on new trends in business. Chris, a professional speaker, was fascinated with Alex's ideas and drove 200 miles to hear him speak. But he fell asleep within 15 minutes of the opening of Alex's presentation, which was delivered in a flat, dull monotone. Alex's voice became a barrier to the vibrancy of his ideas. Little communication occurred.

➤ A world-famous football player and a world-famous golfer shared two distinctions in common. At the peak of their professions, both of them were perceived as giants in highly competitive sports. And both have an abnormally high-pitched voice. This has always been a shock to people who hear them speak for the first time. Their authority suffers because their voices are inconsistent with their images. They do very few voice commercials. With their stature, they could probably increase their income a million dollars a year through speaking endorsements—if they would work on their tone of voice.

➤ A well-known chief executive officer of a steel company gave the dedication to a new building in a major city. He read his speech to about 1,000 people in the bright outdoors. What he did not know was that page 10 of his speech had been inadvertently copied twice. The CEO read it twice. Since he was not paying attention to the words, he did not realize when he was reading it a second time. What was worse, the audience did not realize it either. Only his speechwriter and a smattering of others were aware of this gaffe. The CEO spoke in a monotone. By the time he got to page 10, nobody was really listening, including himself.

➤ Sue and her twin sister were called "the squeaky twins" when they were cheerleaders in high school. Their voices were high-pitched and dramatically stood out even in the middle of a loud, exciting game. Sue began working on improving her voice using exercises similar to those listed later in this section. After just a couple of months, people became aware of the difference in vocal resonance between Sue and her twin sister when they were together.

➤ When a major investment company went public, the executives who spoke at the initial public offering read their prospectus with little vocal energy. The public offering itself generated equally little excitement, even though the figures the executives spoke about were excellent.

Keys to Effective Voice and Vocal Variety

The keys in this section are among the most important tools for making a positive impression with your voice, whether you are speaking to one person or one thousand.

> ➤ **Your Voice Transmits Energy**
>
> The excitement and enthusiasm you feel should be directly conveyed by the sound of your voice. We quickly get in vocal habit patterns that are difficult to change. But they can be changed or relearned. Record your voice to become aware about how much energy, or how little, you transmit to others.

> ➤ **Your Vocal Tone and Quality Can Count for 84% of Your "Message"**
>
> UCLA Professor Mehrabian's research shows that your vocal tone— intonation, resonance, and delivery—accounts for 84% of the believability you have *when people cannot see you*—such as when you talk on the telephone.

> ➤ **The Sounds of One Word**
>
> Subtleties of voice are far greater than we think. We can read an enormous amount into the vocal tone of people on the telephone during the first few seconds. Call someone you know well and listen as they say "hello." You can almost tell their mood by that single word.

> ➤ **The Four Aspects of Voice**
>
> The four components that make up your vocal expression are relaxation, breathing, projection, and resonance. Each can be altered through exercises to expand your vocal effectiveness. All work together to give your voice its unique characteristics.

> ➤ **Use Vocal Variety**
>
> Vocal variety is a great way to keep people interested and involved. Use a "roller coaster"—consciously lift your voice and then let it plummet. This will make you aware of a monotone and get you in the habit of putting variety into your voice.

> ➤ **Don't Read Speeches**
>
> One of the greatest culprits of a monotone delivery in public speaking is reading the speech aloud. Writing, reading, and speaking are different communication mediums. When you speak, simply use notes and outlines of main ideas. Then your mind will have to select words spontaneously. This will force your voice to be active, animated, and natural as you continually think, adapt, and alter your content.

IMPROVING YOUR VOICE AND VOCAL VARIETY

Listed below are several skill development exercises and tips to enhance your voice and vocal variety in the dozens of interpersonal communications you have daily.

1. Emphasize the Right Word

Read the sentence "Now is the time for change" six times, emphasizing a different word each time. Notice the difference in the meaning each time. Emphasis is critical. Experiment with emphasizing the appropriate word in your everyday conversations.

2. The Voice of the Company

Call five companies at random from the phone book and listen to how they answer the phone. Rate them by the vocal tone and quality. How does your organization rate on initial image? And how do you *personally* rate when you answer your telephone?

3. Good and Bad Voices

List five people you know or hear on radio or television with attractive, pleasant vocal deliveries. List five people who have poor vocal deliveries. Analyze why they are good or bad.

4. Record Yourself

The best exercise to develop your vocal skills is to record yourself. Do this as often as possible. Record a telephone conversation, a business meeting, and even a casual conversation with a friend. The most important improvement mechanism for your vocal delivery is audio feedback.

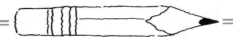

EXERCISE YOUR VOICE

For each of the following exercises, stand, leaning forward in the ready position and maintain a deep, easy breathing pattern throughout.

A. Breathe from the Diaphragm

1. Place your hands on your lower rib cage.

2. Inhale deeply through your nose. The expansion you feel in your lower rib cage is caused by your diaphragm muscle expanding and dropping as the air pushes against it. Your shoulders should not move.

3. Exhale, allowing the air to escape slowly through your slightly open mouth. You will feel a depression around your lower rib cage as the diaphragm rises like a trampoline to support and propel the air.

4. Repeat Steps 1 to 3 several times until you find your rhythm in which breathing is effortless. You should have the sensation of being calm yet full of energy.

5. Do the exercise one more time, moving one hand from the side of your lower rib cage. When you inhale, your breath should push your hand away from the abdominal area. If this does not happen, you are not breathing deeply enough for the diaphragm to do its job.

Remember: While inhaling, the abdominal area should fill up first and more fully than your chest.

B. Add Sound to Your Breathing Exercise

1. Repeat the instructions from the previous exercise, but when you exhale, do it as you say "ah."

2. Relax your jaw, open your mouth, and sustain the "ah" for as long as it is strong and lively. (Do not let yourself run out of air and be sure not to put tension in your throat.)

CONTINUED

C. Tone and Relax Your Head and Neck

1. Relax your jaw so your mouth is slightly open.

2. Slowly drop (don't push) your head to your chest—bring it back to the upright, centered position—drop it to your right shoulder, then back to center—drop it to your left shoulder, then back to center—drop it to the back, return to center.

3. Beginning at center, do two head rolls slowly to the right. Return to center and do two head rolls slowly to the left; return to center.

4. Monitor your breathing throughout; make sure you are not holding your breath. Keep your jaw loose.

D. Tone and Relax Your Shoulders

1. With your hands at your sides, clench your fists.

2. Lift your shoulders to your ears (or try to!).

3. Drop your shoulders and release your fists with a thrust, sighing as you exhale.

E. Tone and Relax Using Shoulder Rolls

1. Do six slow shoulder rolls to the back, keeping your jaw loose. Feel your chest expand; sigh as you exhale.

2. Do six slow shoulder rolls to the front. Sigh as you exhale.

F. Tone and Relax Your Face ("The Prune")

1. Make the "tiniest" face you can. Pucker your lips, close your eyes, and tighten your muscles.

2. Open into the "widest" face you can make.

3. Return to the tight position, and then try to move your entire face (not your head) to the right-hand side.

4. Try to move your face to the left-hand side.

5. Return to the wide position and repeat the exercise.

G. Tone and Relax Your Lips ("The Motorboat")

1. Take a deep breath.

2. Pucker your lips.

3. As you exhale, force the air through your puckered lips. (This will result in a "motorboat" sound and will direct vibrating energy to your lips while relaxing them.)

H. Increase Your Resonance ("King Kong" and "Yawning")

1. Drop your jaw and allow it to hang loosely.

2. Inhale deeply through your nose, allowing your belly to fill up first and more fully than your chest.

   a. As you exhale, say "KING KONG, DING DONG, BING BONG," lowering the tone each time so that the final "BONG" gently eases down into a lower and lower range, until you reach bottom. Do this gently and avoid pushing on your throat muscles.

   b. As you exhale, relax your jaw. Open your mouth wide and allow your throat to open: Start on a high note and lower your pitch gradually until you reach bottom—as when yawning. Do this gently. Avoid pushing on your throat muscles.

I. Project Your Voice

1. Say a test sentence in a conversational tone.

2. Inhale deeply through your nose, allowing your belly to fill first and more fully than your chest.

3. Exhale while saying your test sentence, with the mental image of placing your voice 10 to 20 rows beyond the last row of an imaginary audience.

4. Monitor yourself to make sure you are letting your breath support your voice rather than pushing the sound from your throat.

J. Control and Vary Your Pitch

Say test sentences in a singsong fashion. Play with different pitches and experiment with a range of tones. Song lyrics and poems work well.

K. Practice Your Pacing

Practice test sentences while varying the speed of your delivery between and within them. Insert pauses for additional variety. Record yourself to hear the difference. Read interesting newspaper articles aloud and exaggerate the pace.

All of the preceding exercises need regular practice. As when learning to ride a bicycle, repeat each exercise until it becomes a habit. Whenever possible, practice with a friend.

PERSONAL GOAL WORKSHEET

Determine your answer for each question below and place a check (✓) in the appropriate box. You may not yet know your own communication skills well enough to answer every question, but review the book regularly until you can.

Yes	*No*	
_____	_____	Do you project your voice to others, rather than simply speaking?
_____	_____	Do you know if you have a high nasal or low resonant voice, or somewhere in between?
_____	_____	Are you aware when your voice goes into a monotone, and for what reasons?
_____	_____	Has anyone ever complimented you on your voice? (If so, why? If not, why not?)
_____	_____	Does your telephone voice differ from your speaking voice?
_____	_____	Are you aware of what impact your voice has over the phone?
_____	_____	Do you know how to "put a smile" in your voice?
_____	_____	When you hear a person answer a phone for an organization, do you think about what image is conveyed?

CONTINUED

Now write down three of your habitual patterns in using your voice and vocal variety that you may want to modify, strengthen, or eliminate:

1. _____

_____

2. _____

_____

3. _____

_____

Then write what you plan to practice to modify, strengthen, or change each habit.

1. _____

_____

2. _____

_____

3. _____

_____

Remember: Practice Makes Permanent

Behavioral Skill #6: Language, Nonwords, and Pauses

> 66
> *Perhaps of all of the creations of man, language is the most astonishing.*"

–Lytton Strachey

Language is made of both words and nonwords. People communicate most effectively when they are able to select the right words. This requires a rich vocabulary that can be used responsively and appropriately as the situation demands. You would not talk to a child the same way as to a group of physicists.

Pauses are an integral part of language. An effective communicator uses natural pauses between sentences, and outstanding communicators pause for dramatic effect as well. Nonword fillers such as *um, ah, er, well, okay,* and *you know* are barriers to clear communication.

Behavioral Objective

Your goal in developing your language skills is to *use appropriate and clear language for your listeners.* Work to *replace* irritating, distracting, and undermining "nonwords" with pauses. These will enable you to gather your thoughts and allow your listeners to think about what you are saying.

Examples: Language, Nonwords, and Pauses

➤ Toni is the executive housekeeper of a major hotel chain. She is a big woman with a resonant voice and a confident air. When she talks, she ends every other sentence with "Okay?" Her habit of "asking for agreement" is inconsistent with her natural confidence and the content of her message.

➤ A major government official made a three-minute, eleven-second statement justifying an attack on an enemy position. In that short period there were 57 "um's," "er's," and "ah's." The credibility of his statement was dramatically flawed with these nonword fillers of nervousness.

➤ Kevin is an outstanding speech trainer. At six feet, six inches tall with a booming voice, he is good looking, articulate, and much in demand as a speaker. He also has one distraction. In conversation (as well as in speeches) he often inserts the word "sort of" as a qualifier. This diminishes his credibility, particularly when he is making an emphatic statement. Such qualifiers are ingrained habits that are difficult to break.

Keys to Effective Use of Language and Pauses

The more you build your communication skills, the more aware you become of the importance of the words—or nonwords—you use. The following tips will help you improve your use of language:

> **Use Direct Language**

State and ask for what you want and mean. In her book *Customer Satisfaction: Practical Tools for Building Important Relationships*, Dru Scott emphasizes the difference by recommending you replace "I'll try" with "I will" and "We can't" with "You can." Rather than saying, "I'll try and get an answer for you," replace it with "I will check and get back to you before 4 P.M."

> **Increase Your Vocabulary**

Children increase their vocabulary through formal study at school. As adults we do not have the same motivation because we are not being directly graded. But our education level, clarity, and effectiveness in communications are "graded" daily by the words we use. All of us can increase our vocabulary through the active incorporation of new words.

> **Beware of Jargon**

Jargon is excellent communication shorthand for people who share an occupation or group membership. But even English words will sound like a foreign language if your listener is outside that group and does not understand your jargon.

> **Incorporate More Pauses**

You can pause naturally for three to four seconds, even in the middle of a sentence. The problem is we are not used to doing it. In our own minds, a three- or four-second pause can seem like 20 seconds. Practice pausing and getting feedback to learn how natural you sound when you pause. Push pausing to the limit during practice and you will do it more naturally in real conversations.

> **Replace Nonwords with Pauses**

Some people call them "word whiskers"—fillers such as *um, ah, er, well, okay,* and *you know* that are unnecessary, unwanted, and superfluous barriers to communication. Such nonwords are not only sloppy but also distracting when repeated as a habit. Record yourself or solicit feedback to recognize your nonwords, and then concentrate to eliminate them.

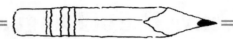

IMPROVING YOUR USE OF LANGUAGE AND PAUSES

Listed below are several skill development exercises and tips to enhance your use of language and pauses in the dozens of interpersonal communications you have daily.

1. Use One New Word a Day

Force yourself to use one new word every day in your conversation. Find a half dozen times when you can use that word. Try words such as: dissemble, jocular, fulsome, empirical, robust, and espouse. The words do not have to be long or intellectual—just different. Make your own list and work at it daily.

2. Use a Dictionary

Put a dictionary at your desk in your office and at home—and use it. Most of us rarely use a dictionary unless it becomes a habit. Just looking up each new word you read or hear will go a long way to increasing your vocabulary. A larger vocabulary gives you the ability to draw on the right word or phrase when appropriate. It does not mean you use big words to show off—simply that you are able to use the clearest, most colorful, most apt word for the situation.

3. Watch Your Jargon

We all have some jargon in our lives. List 10 jargon phrases common to you. Make yourself aware where you use them. It is fine to use them with people who understand what they mean, but they can be alienating or confusing to others.

CONTINUED

4. Incorporate Pauses

Talk into a tape recorder and consciously leave three-second pauses. At first, leave a pause between sentences. Then leave a three- or four-second pause in the middle of a sentence. Exaggerate the pauses so they feel very long to you when you are recording them. Then on playback, listen to how natural they sound.

5. Get Rid of Your Nonwords

You can effectively get rid of nonword fillers through these two simple ways to modify your behavior:

a. Ask an associate or friend to say your name every time you use your habitual nonword. For example, if you tend to use um, then ask your partner to simply state your name every time you say um in a conversation. He should do this without saying anything else. Your name is simply a feedback tool. Very quickly you will become sensitized to your use of that nonword. Before long your mind will stop you before you say it and you will leave a pause as a replacement.

b. Record yourself at every opportunity to sensitize yourself to your nonword. Listening to it over and over will remind you to leave a pause instead of the irritating, distracting nonword that you use. Record yourself just chatting or in formal situations or on the phone—it does not matter. Just be sure to continue the feedback daily.

PERSONAL GOAL WORKSHEET

Determine your answer for each question below and place a check (✓) in the appropriate box. You may not yet know your own communication skills well enough to answer every question, but review the book regularly until you can.

Yes	*No*	
_____	_____	Do you know how long you pause when you are speaking formally?
_____	_____	Does your occupation use jargon?
_____	_____	Do you use slang, code words, or jargon in your normal conversation without realizing it?
_____	_____	Can you recall the last time you looked up a new word in the dictionary?
_____	_____	Do you know the appropriate length of a pause?
_____	_____	Do you use pauses automatically?
_____	_____	Are you able to pause for dramatic effect?
_____	_____	Do you know what the most common nonword is?

CONTINUED

CONTINUED

Now write down three of your habitual patterns in your use of language, nonwords, and pauses that you may want to modify, strengthen, or eliminate:

1. _____
   _____

2. _____
   _____

3. _____
   _____

Then write what you plan to practice to modify, strengthen, or change each habit.

1. _____
   _____

2. _____
   _____

3. _____
   _____

Remember: Practice Makes Permanent

Behavioral Skill #7: Listener Involvement

❝*Your listeners won't care what you say until they know that you care.***❞**

–Anonymous

When you speak and engage a listener at the intellectual level only, you are operating in a narrow range. You are appealing mostly to the linear processing of the left brain. For pure information, this is adequate. Then again, facts and figures can be communicated effectively in writing. Indeed, people can read five times faster than you can speak.

Communicating interpersonally, on the other hand, involves ideas and opinions. You are trying to move people to action or persuade them to agree. If you miss engaging your listeners' right brains, you are missing much of your potential for impact.

Behavioral Objective

Your goal in developing your listener-involvement skills is to *maintain the active interest of each person with whom you are communicating*, every time you talk— whether to one person or one thousand.

Examples: Listener Involvement

➤ Richard is a pastor who skillfully uses humor to keep people awake, involved, and interested during his sermons. One morning he added something else. He held up an Etch A Sketch® toy and wrote "SIN" on the surface. As he described how the Lord "wiped the slate clean" of sin, the pastor did the same on his prop to show a blank surface. There wasn't one person who did not get the message.

➤ Shawna was called in to the president's office for a meeting. She was on friendly terms with him and waltzed into the office casually. When the president got up and closed the door before saying a word, she knew the tone of this meeting was different. She was involved.

➤ Frank is a good speaker and usually keeps people's attention in the training sessions he leads. But after lunch, people tend to get sleepy, so Frank often combines two behavioral skills—movement and eye communication—when he sees someone begin to nod off. He walks over toward the "nodder," out of his normal movement range. This changes the room dynamics. As the nodder looks up, Frank looks at that person. The nodder gets energized by the eye contact and leaps to alertness.

➤ Stewart gave his first Toastmasters speech, which club members call an icebreaker. He placed on the lectern a large object covered by a heavy cloth. Before he said a word, he took out a hammer from underneath the lectern, whipped off the covering to reveal a slab of ice, and began hammering at it saying, "This is my icebreaker." His audience became involved.

Keys to Effective Listener Involvement

Whether just one person in a conversation or a thousand people in an audience, listeners are bombarded by stimuli every instant. You must engage all of their senses and their entire mind. The more involved your listeners are, the more you can convince them of your message.

Engaging Listeners with "Swirls"

A "swirl" is an instant of a listener's total involvement. A swirl can come from laughing, sensing an "aha" moment, being invited to the front to do an exercise, having to think of a question, deciding whether to volunteer, and the like.

Many swirls are created through humor and humanization, but they can come from any of the *nine listener-involving techniques* listed below. The nine techniques center around three areas: style, interaction, and content, as follows:

Style	Interaction	Content
Drama	Questions	Interest
Eye Communication	Demonstrations	Humor
Movement	Samples/Gimmicks	
Visuals		

All of these techniques can be adapted to large groups or to individual communication. The next sections provide examples of each technique.

Involving Listeners with Your Speaking Style

As a speaker, your action to involve your listeners could be as slight as moving into an audience or using a different type of visual aid. Or you could do something more substantial, as in the following examples.

Drama

➤ Create a strong opening by announcing a serious problem, telling a moving story, or asking a rhetorical question to get each person thinking. You can also make a startling statement.

➤ Include a dramatic element such as a long pause to emphasize a key statement, vocal tone and pitch changes, or higher-intensity emotions such as anger, joy, sadness or excitement.

➤ Add visual and kinesthetic detail such as color, smell, temperature, and other sensations to vividly recreate a story or experience for your listener(s).

➤ End your communication with a dramatic or inspirational quote, or firm call to action.

Eye Communication

➤ Survey all of your listeners when you start speaking before beginning extended eye communication with any individual.

➤ Keep your listeners involved and engaged by maintaining three- to six-second contact with as many as possible. Do not forget "orphans" at the far edges of a room or along your side of a conference table.

➤ Gauge the reaction of your listeners throughout your presentation. Do they agree? Are they bored? Do they have questions?

Movement

➤ Change the dynamics of your presentation with purposeful movement. Whenever possible, move around.

➤ Never back away from your listener(s). Move toward them—especially at the beginning and the end of your communication.

Visuals

➤ Add variety by using visuals. Give your listener(s) something to look at in addition to you.

➤ Use different types of visual aids in a formal presentation, such as both overheads and flip charts. Rehearse to make your transitions smooth and non-distracting.

➤ Get on-the-spot listener participation by experimenting with techniques such as writing listener concerns on a flip chart or filling in an overhead transparency as you go.

Involving Listeners Through Interaction

Interactivity fosters a sense of collaboration between you and your listeners. The following techniques will encourage your listeners to interact with you.

Questions

There are three types of questions you can use in a group setting. Each allows you to obtain a deeper level of involvement:

➤ Ask rhetorical questions to keep your listeners active and thinking, especially when you do not have time or it is not appropriate to discuss an issue.

➤ Ask for a show of hands to get listeners more involved and to give you a quick way to gauge their reactions.

➤ Ask for a volunteer. Even though only one person will speak or act, you can feel the adrenaline rush through the others as they consider whether they might be the volunteer.

Demonstrations

➤ Plan ahead for every step or procedure and be sure to accurately time the demonstration before you use it.

➤ Have a volunteer from the group help you in your demonstration.

Samples/Gimmicks

➤ Have fun with your listeners. Get them involved yet always stay in control of the session. Keep things appropriate for your profession as well as for your listeners.

➤ If you are promoting a product, consider using samples of it to reward volunteer participants.

➤ Use creativity. Gimmicks can be used effectively in most business settings. But keep things in good taste.

Involving Listeners with Content

Sometimes *what* you say can be as effective in involving your listeners as how you say it. Consider the following points of content:

Interest

➤ Before you speak, review what you plan to say by asking yourself, "How will I benefit my listeners?"

➤ Remember short attention spans. Use eye contact to gauge interest. Use examples, drama, humor, visuals, and movement to engage your listener.

➤ Maintain a high level of personal interest. If you make the same presentation repeatedly, consider changing examples, getting listeners involved in different places, or changing the order of your presentation to maintain your enthusiasm.

Humor

➤ Begin with a friendly, warm comment. A personal remark will start the ball rolling and relax things.

➤ Make your humor appropriate to your listeners and relevant to your point of view. Be professional while allowing your "humanness" to appear.

➤ Develop a sense of humor and use it. Tell stories, refer to current events, include one-liners, poke fun at yourself, or even play off listeners' comments.

➤ If you "lay an egg," stand back and admire it! Be willing to laugh at yourself.

IMPROVING YOUR
LISTENER-INVOLVEMENT SKILLS

Listed below are several skill development exercises and tips to enhance your listener-involvement skills in the dozens of interpersonal communications you have daily.

1. Learn from the TV Masters

Watch the TV talk show hosts and notice how they continually involve their listeners and their guests. They move around; ask questions; engage individuals with eye communication; and use gimmicks, props, visuals, and humor. Professionals use the same skills presented in this book.

2. Follow a Question with Another Question

A popular spontaneity exercise, which is often used as a sales technique for "discovery," also can be used to involve any listener in any setting. It involves asking a question and then following up with another question. Here's how it goes:

Focus on what you want to know about the person with whom you are talking, and then ask the person a question about that subject. Most people will just answer and stop. Use their answer to trigger another question, geared toward the subject area you want to pursue. Often this will get the other person engaged in also asking you questions, which leads to an involved interaction. Respond to any question asked, but while you are talking, think of the next question you want to ask. Your mind can think at the same time you are talking, and you can move a conversation wherever you want it to go.

This technique can be practiced anywhere. It is effective at dinner parties and other formal settings. A memorable Dale Carnegie story is from a time he sat next to a wealthy matron at a dinner party and spent the entire night asking her questions about her life. At the end of the evening she said, "What an interesting conversationalist you are, Mr. Carnegie." But Carnegie had never talked about himself at all.

3. Do It Daily

Take each of the nine listener-involving techniques and apply one each day in your business life. When you finish the cycle of nine, start again so that every day you are aware of making an effort to involve people. It will not be long before this becomes a positive habit.

PERSONAL GOAL WORKSHEET

Determine your answer for each question below and place a check (✓) in the appropriate box. You may not yet know your own communication skills well enough to answer every question, but review the book regularly until you can.

Yes   *No*

_____ _____ Do you know the three different forms of questions?

_____ _____ Do you physically move around when you are in a speaking situation?

_____ _____ Are you aware of the need to engage your audience's right brain?

_____ _____ If you are presenting a lot of information, do you obtain regular feedback signals by involving your audience?

_____ _____ Do you know the two most important elements of your content to involve a listener when you are talking?

CONTINUED

Now write down three of your habitual patterns in your listener-involvement skills that you may want to modify, strengthen, or eliminate:

1. _____

   _____

2. _____

   _____

3. _____

   _____

Then write what you plan to practice to modify, strengthen, or change each habit.

1. _____

   _____

2. _____

   _____

3. _____

   _____

Remember: Practice Makes Permanent

Behavioral Skill #8: Humor

> **"** *The man who causes them to laugh gets more votes for the measure than the man who forces them to think."*

—Malcolm de Chazall

Humor is one of the most important skills for effective interpersonal communication, yet one of the most elusive. Some people are naturally personable and likable. Others have to work at it. Humor is a learnable skill and we can all learn to use this important tool more effectively.

Behavioral Objective

Your goal in developing your humor skills is to *create a bond between yourself and your listeners*. Your use of humor will enable them to enjoy listening to you more. Humor can make you more "human" and help others have a good time when they are around you.

Examples: Humor

➤ Beverly, the founder of a large retail outlet, is well known in the retail industry. She is also a wife and mother of two children. She was once asked at a news conference whether she would serve as a director on her company's board. Her reply: "I don't do boards or windows."

➤ John is a professional speaker who used to be a successful football coach. When he just missed taking his team to the national championships, the owner fired him. Shortly after that, John was set to give a speech and was introduced with a flowery introduction that neglected to mention what everybody already knew. He ad-libbed his opening: "You know I used to be the coach of the Kings but I got fired. I was fired because of illness and fatigue. The fans were sick and tired of me."

➤ Every day Sunny calls her mother, who is in a nursing home. One of Sunny's goals in every phone call is to make her mother laugh somehow. She is always able to succeed.

➤ The most memorable incident in the 1984 U.S. presidential debates was Ronald Reagan's humorous response to a question about his advanced age. He answered that he would not make a campaign issue of his opponent Walter Mondale's "youth and inexperience." Often the most vivid memories from the presidential debates are comments that were made in humor or jest.

Keys to Effective Use of Humor

Some of the most effective swirls come from moments of lightness or involvement. Those emotional moments are the best time to get your message through. You reach both the right brain and the left brain when you use humor and humanization. The following tips will help you develop your use of humor:

➤ **Don't Tell Jokes**

About one in 100 persons is a good teller of jokes, but 10 times that number think they can tell jokes well. Unless you are really effective at pacing, delivery, and style, do not try telling jokes in formal situations.

➤ **Do Tell Stories and Anecdotes**

We are funny, humorous, and human when we open ourselves to be vulnerable—to be part of the human comedy. Much can be gained in interpersonal communications in sharing humorous asides, stories, anecdotes, or reactions.

➤ **Humanization Is Humor**

In most interpersonal communications, comedy is not really the goal. Instead, we want to connect on the personal level with our listeners. That connection is most often made through likeability. This quality comes from such factors as being personal, open, friendly, caring, interested, personable, emotional, concerned, pleasant, comfortable, confident, unselfish, feeling, and fun.

➤ **Remember the Personality Factor**

People often vote for political leaders on the basis of likeability. Others decide whether they agree with you or support your position based on personality. Both factors are most characterized by the humor or humanization that you project.

➤ *Your Smile Is What People See*

When we are talking, people look at our face. Our predominant feature is our smile. This important feature shows quickly whether we are excited, enthused, angry, serious, or some combination of these. Our sense of humor is largely perceived nonverbally through a smile. It is important to know your natural "smileability."

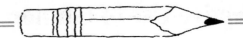

IMPROVING YOUR USE OF HUMOR

Listed below are several skill development exercises and tips to enhance your use of humor in the dozens of interpersonal communications you have daily.

1. Determine What Makes You Laugh

Find out more about your sense of humor. Do you have a dry wit, or do you like earthy stories? Do you have an infectious laugh, or do you exhibit an easy smile? Everybody is different, yet most of us love to laugh and have fun. Find out what your "humor profile" is. Ask others to rate your sense of humor on a scale of one to 10.

2. Make Someone Laugh

People can consciously use humor. In a few seconds, one person can make another person (or a group of people) laugh, smile, chuckle, chortle, or relax—if they work at it. If you make humor a conscious goal, then with everything that passes through your mind, you will automatically look for the connection that relates to the human comedy.

3. Think Funny

People who laugh easily tend to filter their world through a screen of humor. They look for the bright side rather than the dark side. They can turn a crisis into an opportunity. Think "funny" on a conscious level. Take your subject seriously but do not take yourself seriously. You will be surprised at how this conscious effort will enable you to be more spontaneous, open, and fun.

 CONTINUED

4. Gain Awareness Through Feedback

Record yourself in every formal presentation you give. Make a conscious effort to use humor in your talk and then check the audience feedback to see how it worked. Count the laughs, chuckles, and smiles that you are able to generate from your audience.

5. Watch Others

We all know people we enjoy being around. We want to be with them because they are fun, light, and lively. Search these people out. See how they involve others. These people are not necessarily comics or jokesters, but individuals who continually create swirls in their interpersonal communications. Experiment with trying some of their habits and adapting them to your style.

6. Keep a Humor Journal

In a journal or diary, keep a page for quotes, quips, anecdotes, stories, and "funny things" that happen in your daily life. Do this for a week, noting 10 "light" items in your life each day. If you do not have 10 a day, work harder at humor. Life is meant to be joyful.

PERSONAL GOAL WORKSHEET

Determine your answer for each question below and place a check (✓) in the appropriate box. You may not yet know your own communication skills well enough to answer every question, but review the book regularly until you can.

Yes	*No*	
_____	_____	Are you funny? Do you laugh at yourself?
_____	_____	Do you know the estimated percentage of people who know how to tell jokes well?
_____	_____	Do you tell more than two jokes a week?
_____	_____	Do people tend to laugh when they are around you?
_____	_____	Do you know what makes you laugh?

CONTINUED

Now write down three of your habitual patterns in your use of humor that you may want to modify, strengthen, or eliminate:

1. _____

   _____

2. _____

   _____

3. _____

   _____

Then write what you plan to practice to modify, strengthen, or change each habit.

1. _____

   _____

2. _____

   _____

3. _____

   _____

Remember: Practice Makes Permanent

Behavioral Skill #9: The Natural Self

When we encounter a natural style, we are always surprised and delighted, for we thought to see an author and found a man."

–Pascal

Think of the most forceful speaker you know. Think of the most impressive leader you know. In each case, you will not find one who is a copy of anybody else. We each are different—each with our own strengths and weaknesses. Although this is a simple concept, it gains complexity when you consider the thousands of variables in interpersonal communications. We have resources to draw on—natural strengths that are already there as well as areas to make into strengths.

Behavioral Objective

Your goal in developing your natural self is to *be authentic*. Work to be yourself in all communication circumstances, understanding and using your natural strengths and building communication weaknesses into strengths. To be your natural self, have the confidence in your mental spontaneity to adapt to circumstances.

Example: The Natural Self

In an isolated area of Italy is a small town surrounded by mountains with craggy cliffs and caves. People moved into these caves and lived by themselves in isolated and primitive circumstances. Over time they came to be looked on with disdain by the town dwellers, even though the hermit "cave colony" did no harm.

One year a cruel young man named Simon began work at the town foundry. He organized a gang that regularly harassed the cave people. After a few years of abuse, something unusual happened.

On a quiet Sunday morning, a cave dweller named Rolando came down from the hills. He calmly walked to the town square and began speaking. He was dressed in scraggly clothes. He did not have formal schooling or social graces. But he spoke confidently with conviction. A crowd gathered. Rolando asked why the peaceful cave dwellers were being persecuted. He described their lives in the cave and the unhappiness that Simon and his gang caused.

Although Rolando had a simple vocabulary, he held the crowd enthralled with his message as he spoke from his heart. He was a natural. From that day on, harassing of the cave dwellers stopped.

Keys to Being Your Natural Self

Being your natural self is an attitude that involves (1) acknowledging your strengths and your weak areas, and (2) converting your weaknesses into strengths. It is as much a behavioral skill as the eight you have already read about, as follows:

1. Eye Communication

2. Posture and Movement

3. Gestures and Facial Expressions

4. Dress and Appearance

5. Voice and Vocal Variety

6. Language, Nonwords, and Pauses

7. Listener Involvement

8. Humor

From these eight skills, list below the three that reflect your greatest strengths, with the first being your strongest skill:

_____

_____

_____

List the three behavioral skills that are weaknesses for you, with the weakest first:

_____

_____

_____

Learning like a Juggler

If you ever learned to juggle, you probably learned to start with one ball first just to get the rhythm. Then you added a second ball to practice with both hands working together. Finally, you practiced adding a third ball until you could juggle.

Becoming an expert in interpersonal communications is much like juggling. You master one skill at a time and add to them once they become habits.

A good start is to acknowledge your natural strengths and be thankful you do not have to learn them from scratch. Realize that many others do. You may have an easy, natural smile while others have to work at lightening up in their interpersonal communications. On the other hand, you may find it difficult to gesture naturally, while someone else might have been born effusive. Acknowledge your strengths and work to improve and capitalize on them.

Next, work on your weaknesses, one at a time, until you convert them to strengths. Take your weakest area first and concentrate on improving it every day for a week. For example, if eye communication is a difficult skill for you, put your conscious mental energy into developing extended eye communication each day for a week or two. Then move to another skill. Continue this process until you have gone through all nine skills.

Communicating Well Is a Lifetime Process

No one is a completed, effective communicator. We always find new unwanted habits that pop up, as well as old undesirable habits that creep back. We also find new strengths as we mature and as we experiment with various behavioral skills.

Often a newfound habit will work to improve an old habit. Or two habits will work together to form an effective new behavior. For example, movement and extended eye communication can breed confidence that allows a person to maintain excellent eye communication with a listener. It may even allow reaching out and touching the listener's arm.

Remember that interpersonal communication involves a multitude of skills. And all skills can be learned and practiced.

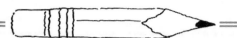

DISCOVERING YOUR NATURAL SELF

Listed below are two skill development exercises and tips for helping you analyze your strengths and weaknesses and find out if your analysis matches others' impressions of you.

1. Show five people the list of the nine behavioral skills and ask each person to rank you, from your greatest strength to your greatest weakness. Observe what others see in you. Compare the responses and your self-perceptions. If they match, you know where to start work. If they do not, take those areas that are least consistent and work on them first.

2. Ask three people to fill out in detail a Coaching Feedback Sheet (such as the one on the next page) about you after your next presentation.

COACHING FEEDBACK SHEET

	Excellent	Good	Needs Work	Comments
Overall Impression				
Appearance				
Enthusiasm				
Posture				
Expressions				
Content				
Opening				
Listener Involvement				
Word Pictures				
Examples/Quotes				
Lack of Jargon				
Closing				
Delivery Skills				
Extended Eye Contact				
Natural Gestures				
Use of Nonwords				
Pauses				
Voice				
Natural Movement				
Humor				
Visual Aids				

(This form may be copied without further permission.)

PERSONAL GOAL WORKSHEET

Determine your answer for each question below and place a check (✓) in the appropriate box. You may not yet know your own communication skills well enough to answer every question, but review the book regularly until you can.

Yes   *No*

_____   _____   Are you comfortable speaking in any of these situations—to a small group, to a large audience, in a high-pressure one-on-one sales situation?

_____   _____   Do you know in which of the four stages of speaking you normally reside?

_____   _____   Do you know what behavioral changes you experience during high-stress communications?

_____   _____   Do you know your three strongest communication skill areas?

_____   _____   What about your three weakest communication areas?

_____   _____   Can you list your strengths and weaknesses?

CONTINUED

Now write down three of your habitual patterns in your natural self that you may want to modify, strengthen, or eliminate:

1. _____

   _____

2. _____

   _____

3. _____

   _____

Then write what you plan to practice to modify, strengthen, or change each habit.

1. _____

   _____

2. _____

   _____

3. _____

   _____

Remember: Practice Makes Permanent

A P P E N D I X

Creating a Communication "Experience"

Think of communication not as an interaction, but an experience you have with another person or a group of people. As you develop your behavioral skills for more interpersonal effectiveness, the changes you make in your communication habits are likely to have an impact—a positive one.

What can you do to create an "experience" with another person or a group? Apply these tips:

➤ **Exhibit confident behavior.** Without expressing confidence in your interactions, all else will be lost.

➤ **Put yourself in their shoes.** What will stand out for them in the interaction? What is in it for them if they have a positive experience?

➤ **Think *story*.**[1] We all love to hear a story, and we relate to stories by "experiencing" them. Use stories in your communications. Use word pictures, metaphors, props, and quotes. Make your communications live and breathe.

➤ **Think of the senses.** All five senses connect to the first brain. The visual and auditory are most dominant, so use them with great expression to allow your listener to experience you. And when you can, go beyond to the other senses—touch, taste, and smell. This will require more creativity, but you can do it. (For example, if you have a small office, have chocolate chip cookies for your clients. Meet over a meal rather than in your office. For a speech have candy on the chairs. Shake hands warmly with two hands rather than one.)

➤ **Expand your framework** to enlarge the communication experience.

---

[1] For more information on communicating through stories, read *Making Your Message Memorable,* by Deborah Shouse, Ron Zoglin, and Susan Fenner, Ph.D., a Crisp Series book.

Influencing Others Through Six Leadership Skills

Great leaders are great communicators, and great communicators can become leaders in their own spheres of influence. Through communicating effectively, leaders are able to exert influence.

There are six skills of leadership that can be learned and improved with intention and practice. All are related to how we communicate and relate to others. Three of them specifically depend on the ability to communicate effectively.

Mastering the following six skills will put you in the mind-set of a leader and will set you up for greatest success and influence:

Individual Characteristics

Leaders have and look for:

> ➤ Forward lean—Leaders are communicators. Their energy and people skills enable them to exert influence.

> ➤ Character—Leaders have ethics, integrity, trustworthiness, and humility. Leaders care and consider the organization first. Leaders are not sarcastic.

> ➤ Savvy—Leaders are intelligent, street-smart, conceptual, and tactical. They have an entrepreneurial spirit, yet they are good managers.

Team (Organization, Group) Actions

Leaders do:

> ➤ Communicate a clear vision—Leaders are passionate about where they want the group to go, and they continually articulate and repeat the vision—up, down, and laterally.

> ➤ Mobilize resources—Leaders know what they need to get the job done through others, and they continually assemble and motivate the resources required.

> ➤ Manage (self and others) through measurements—What you measure is what you get. Leaders manage themselves first by high and specific standards and motivate others through measurements.

Review: The Nine Behavioral Skills for Effective Interpersonal Communication

Vocal delivery and the visual elements, as well as personality, likeability, and openness are the primary ingredients of communication skills for leaders.

For your review, the specific behavioral characteristics and traits that make up these important ingredients are the following:

1. Eye Communication: to look sincerely and steadily at another person

2. Posture and Movement: to stand tall and move naturally and easily

3. Gestures and Facial Expressions: to be relaxed and natural when you speak

4. Dress and Appearance: to dress, groom, and appear appropriate for the environment you are in, as well as for yourself

5. Voice and Vocal Variety: to use your voice as a rich, resonant instrument

6. Language, Nonwords, and Pauses: to use appropriate and clear language for your listeners, replacing nonwords with pauses

7. Listener Involvement: to maintain the active interest and involvement of each person with whom you are communicating

8. Using Humor: to create a bond between yourself and your listeners

9. The Natural Self: to be authentic

Communicating is a learnable skill. It takes work, but the results are worth it. With practice you can raise this skill to an art form, and even enjoy the process.

Remember, Practice Makes Permanent!

Additional Reading

Bozek, Phillip. *50 One-Minute Tips to Better Communication.* Crisp Series, 1998.

Caroselli, Marlene. *Thinking On Your Feet.* Crisp Series, 1992.

Chapman, Elwood N. and Wil McKnight. *Attitude*: Your Most Priceless Possession. Crisp Series, 2002.

Decker, Bert. *Creating Messages That Motivate.* San Francisco: Just Write Books, 2005.

Decker, Bert. *You've Got To Be Believed To Be Heard.* NY: St. Martin's Press, 1992.

Gladwell, Malcolm. *Blink.* NY: Little, Brown and Company, 2005.

Goleman, Daniel. *Emotional Intelligence.* NY: Bantam, 1997.

Goleman, Daniel, Richard Boyatzis, and Annie McKee. *Primal Leadership.* Boston, MA: Harvard Business School Press, 2002.

Kravitz, S. Michael and Susan D. Schubert. *Emotional Intelligence Works.* Crisp Series, 2000.

Lencioni, Patrick. *Death by Meeting.* San Francisco: Jossey-Bass, 2004.

Manning, Marilyn and Patricia Haddock. *Developing as a Professional.* Crisp Series, 2004.

Paulson, Terry. *Making Humor Work.* Crisp Series, 1989.

Shouse, Deborah, Ron Zoglin, and Susan Fenner. *Making Your Message Memorable.* Crisp Series, 2003.

Zuker, Elaina. *Creating Rapport.* Crisp Series, 2005.

NOTES

NOTES

NOTES

NOTES

NOTES

AlsoAvailable

Books • Videos • CD-ROMs • Computer-Based Training Products

> If you enjoyed this book, we have great news for you. There are more than 200 books available in the *Crisp Fifty-Minute™ Series*. For more information visit us online at:
> www.courseilt.com

Subject Areas Include:

Management

Human Resources

Communication Skills

Personal Development

Sales/Marketing

Finance

Coaching and Mentoring

Customer Service/Quality

Small Business and Entrepreneurship

Training

Life Planning

Writing